MW00762427

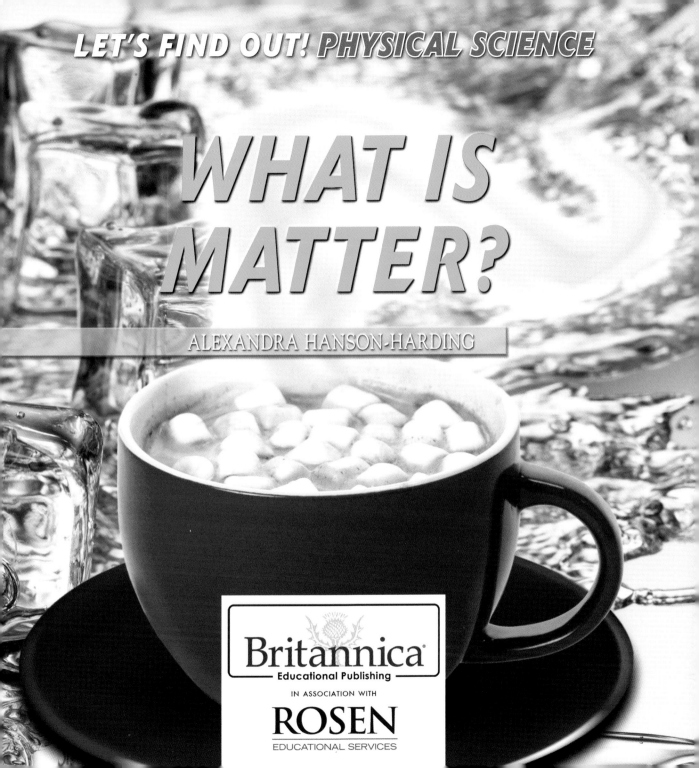

WHAT IS MATTER?

ALEXANDRA HANSON-HARDING

Britannica
Educational Publishing

IN ASSOCIATION WITH

ROSEN
EDUCATIONAL SERVICES

Published in 2015 by Britannica Educational Publishing (a trademark of Encyclopædia Britannica, Inc.) in association with The Rosen Publishing Group, Inc.
29 East 21st Street, New York, NY 10010

Copyright © 2015 The Rosen Publishing Group, Inc., and Encyclopædia Britannica, Inc. Encyclopaedia Britannica, Britannica, and the Thistle logo are registered trademarks of Encyclopædia Britannica, Inc. All rights reserved.

Distributed exclusively by Rosen Publishing.
To see additional Britannica Educational Publishing titles, go to rosenpublishing.com.

First Edition

Britannica Educational Publishing
J.E. Luebering: Director, Core Reference Group
Mary Rose McCudden: Editor, Britannica Student Encyclopedia

Rosen Publishing
Hope Lourie Killcoyne: Executive Editor
Nelson Sá: Art Director
Nicole Russo: Designer
Cindy Reiman: Photography Manager
Marty Levick: Photo Researcher

Cataloging-in-Publication Data

Hanson-Harding, Alexandra, author.
What is matter?/Alexandra Hanson-Harding. — First edition.
    pages cm — (Let's find out! Physical science)
Includes bibliographical references and index.
Audience: Grades 3-6.
ISBN 978-1-62275-487-8 (library bound) — ISBN 978-1-62275-489-2 (pbk.) — ISBN 978-1-62275-490-8 (6-pack)
1. Matter—Juvenile literature. I. Title.
QC173.16.H37 2015
530—dc23

2014001082

Manufactured in the United States of America

Photo credits:
Cover, p. 1 (cocoa) © iStockphoto.com/bmcent1; cover, p. 1 (steam, saucer) ecco/Shutterstock.com; cover, interior pages (background) gennady/Shutterstock.com; p. 4 gualbertobecerra/iStock/Thinkstock; pp. 5, 20, 22 Encyclopædia Britannica, Inc.; p. 6 Eugene Sergeev/Shutterstock.com; pp. 6–7 © Comstock/Thinkstock; pp. 8–9 AleksVF/iStock /Thinkstock; p. 9 Ned Frisk/Blend Images/Getty Images; p. 10 Joe Kohen/WireImage/Getty Images; pp. 10–11 Dorling Kindersley/Vetta/Getty Images; p. 12 Stefania Rossitto/Shutterstock.com; p. 13 David Chasey/Photodisc/Getty Images; p. 14 dmitriyGo/Shutterstock.com; p. 15 Yevgen Royik/Hemera/Thinkstock; p. 16 McCarony/Shutterstock.com; p. 17 Fritz Goro/Time & Life Pictures/Getty Images; pp. 18–19 © AP Images; p. 19 Science Picture Co/Getty Images; p. 21 Science and Society Picture Library/Getty Images; p. 23 doomu/Shutterstock.com; p. 24 © Photos.com/Thinkstock; p. 25 Mark Herreid/Shutterstock.com; p. 26 Tony Bowler/Shutterstock.com; p. 27 © Photos.com/Jupiter Images; pp. 28–29 @ Daniel Yip Go/Flickr/Getty Images; p. 29 Sharon Montrose/Iconica/Getty Images.

CONTENTS

Matter Matters

Anything that takes up space is called matter. Air, water, rocks, and people are examples of matter. All matter is made up of tiny particles, or bits, called atoms. One way of describing different types of matter is by their mass. The mass of an object is the amount of material that makes up the object. A bowling ball, for example, is heavy. It has more mass than

Some objects are more dense than others. Their particles are more closely crowded together.

A beach ball is much easier to carry than a bowling ball because the beach ball contains much less matter.

a beach ball, which is filled with gas. Even though they are nearly the same size, the bowling ball is harder to carry because it has more mass than the beach ball.

Matter exists in several different forms, called states. The three most familiar states are solid, liquid, and gas.

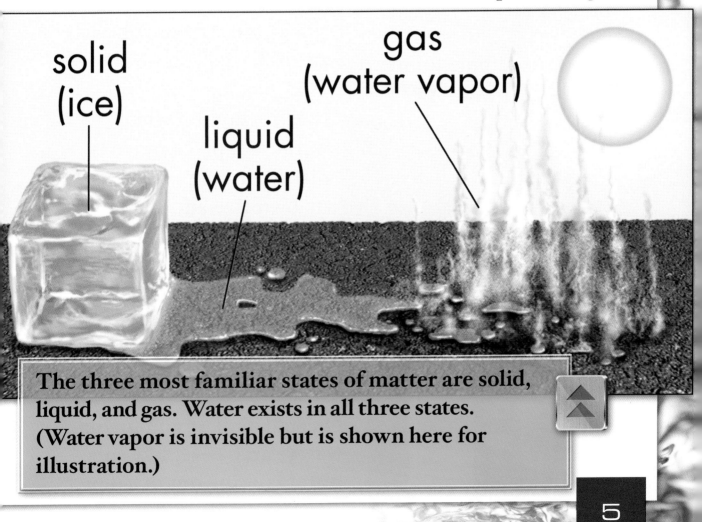

solid
(ice)

liquid
(water)

gas
(water vapor)

The three most familiar states of matter are solid, liquid, and gas. Water exists in all three states. (Water vapor is invisible but is shown here for illustration.)

Rock Solid

On freezing days, a pail of water left outdoors turns to solid ice. Certain things are true of ice that are true of all solids. For example, ice is colder than its liquid form, water. If a piece of ice is placed in a cup, it keeps its own size and shape. Other solids, including rocks, books, and even individual grains of table salt, keep their size and shape, too.

On cold days, even flowing water can freeze, like this water coming out of a pipe.

The constant motion of atoms creates **electromagnetic forces**. This motion creates waves of energy that pull other particles closer or push them away.

The atoms that form solids are held in place by an electromagnetic force. This is a force that pulls atoms close to their neighbors. The atoms always vibrate, or shake. But they stay in a set position, packed close together.

Ice keeps its size and shape. Its atoms are tightly packed together, thanks to electromagnetism.

Liquids: Let It Pour

Milk, paint, and water are examples of liquids. A liquid's shape depends on its container. Otherwise, it just runs all over. For example, milk changes shape when a person pours it from a carton into a glass. But the amount of milk stays the same. Liquid matter has a set volume. Volume is a way to measure the amount of space that matter takes up.

Paint spilled on the floor will spread out, but it keeps its same volume.

Liquids can take different shapes. The thin trickle from the milk carton will fill the glass.

Surface tension is a force that helps create the surface of a liquid. It is caused when surface atoms are attracted, or pulled, to each other.

As with solids, electromagnetic forces also attract atoms in liquids to each other. But the atoms are farther apart. There are fewer of them in the same space. That gives particles the freedom to slip around each other but still stick together.

GASES: SCATTERED MATTER

The air and the helium used to fill balloons are examples of gases. Gas does not have either a set size or a set shape. The average distance between gas atoms is extremely large compared with their tiny size. So the attracting

The helium that fills this Spider-Man parade balloon is lighter than air.

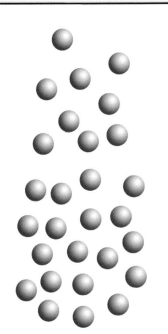

THINK ABOUT IT

Matter in the gaseous state does not have either a set size or a set shape. It can expand to fill a large container, or it can be squeezed into a smaller container.

Atoms of a solid, a liquid, and a gas (*left to right*). Gas atoms move around a container until they run into a wall or another atom.

forces in a gas are weak. Many gases, such as nitrogen and oxygen, float freely around our atmosphere.

Gas fills the entire volume of a container, unlike liquids or solids. If you put gas into a container, the atoms move freely until they hit the wall or another atom. Even though gases are often invisible, they still have mass, like all matter.

MATTER CAN CHANGE: LET'S GET PHYSICAL

All matter has physical properties, which can be measured without changing its composition. Properties such as boiling point,

THINK ABOUT IT

The melting points of different kinds of matter range from -457.6°F (-272°C) for helium to greater than 6,332°F (3,500°C) for carbon in the form of diamond.

The solid rocks in this area have different physical properties, such as color.

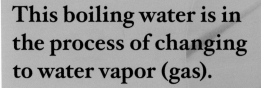

This boiling water is in the process of changing to water vapor (gas).

color, and smell are different for each kind of matter. For example, matter can change from one state to another at different temperatures.

Heat makes liquid water evaporate, or turn into water vapor—a gas. Liquid turns into a gas at a certain temperature, called its boiling point. The water vapor will become liquid again when it's cooled. Cooled down to 32°F (0°C), its freezing point, water will become solid ice. When ice is heated, it begins to melt at the same temperature.

MATTER CAN CHANGE: LET'S GET CHEMICAL

All matter also has chemical properties. A chemical property tells how matter will change under special conditions. For example, iron turns to rust if it's left out in the rain. Paper and wood burn to ashes if they touch a flame. Burning and rusting are called chemical reactions.

These rusting tools are going through a chemical change as they are exposed to the rain.

Chemists study the substances that make up matter. They also create new substances, including fibers, building materials, and medicines, from simpler chemicals.

Glass is normally solid, but it can melt at high temperatures.

Chemical changes are important in many industrial processes. Oil, for example, can be changed to make plastic. Sand can be made into glass. When a material is changed but can still change back to its former state, it is said to have had a reversible change. If the change cannot be undone, it is called an irreversible change.

THE ATTRACTIVE ATOM

Atoms are the basic building blocks of matter. Each atom is made of smaller particles—electrons, protons, and neutrons. These are called subatomic particles. At the center of an atom is a nucleus. The nucleus contains protons and neutrons stuck together. Protons carry a positive electrical charge, while neutrons have no electrical charge. Surrounding the nucleus is a cloud of negatively charged electrons.

Each type of atom has a different

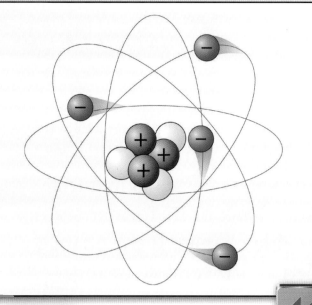

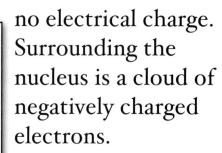

This simple model of an atom shows protons (red), neutrons (white), and electrons (blue).

number of protons. This is known as its atomic number. The atomic number determines what kind of atom it is. For instance, hydrogen has an atomic number of 1 because every hydrogen atom has one proton in its nucleus.

THINK ABOUT IT
Scientists believe that protons and neutrons are made up of even smaller particles. These particles are called quarks.

This image shows a hydrogen atom.

Elementary Elements

An atom is the smallest unit of a chemical element. A chemical element is a basic substance. It cannot be broken down into simpler substances. Ninety-two elements are found in nature. Scientists have created more than twenty additional elements.

Every element has its own symbol. The symbol for some elements is the first letter of their name. For

Think About It

Hydrogen is the most common element in the universe. Hydrogen is a gas.

Dr. Glenn Seaborg discovered ten of the elements on the periodic table, including plutonium.

He is the symbol for helium, the second-most-common element in the universe.

example, H is the symbol for hydrogen and O is the symbol for oxygen. Other elements have a symbol with two letters. For example, He is the symbol for helium and Cl is the symbol for chlorine.

Elements: On the Table

The periodic table is a system for arranging the elements. It arranges the elements in rows (left to right) and columns (top to bottom). In the rows, the elements

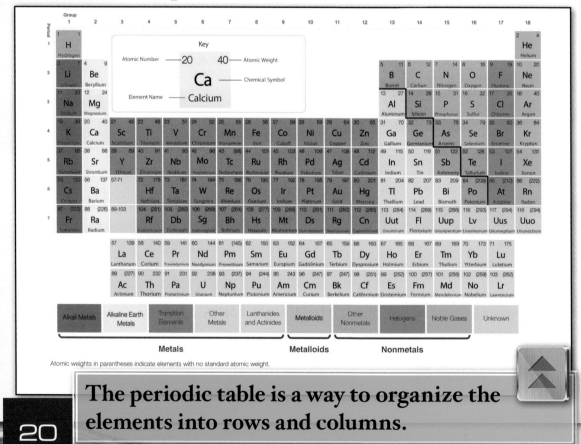

Atomic weights in parentheses indicate elements with no standard atomic weight.

The periodic table is a way to organize the elements into rows and columns.

are placed in order of their atomic number. The columns form groups of elements that have similar chemical properties. For example, certain gases are in one column and metals are in another. The periodic table helps chemists think about the elements and their properties.

COMPARE AND CONTRAST

Look at the elements across the periodic table. How are they different? How are they alike?

Russian chemist Dmitry Mendeleyev developed the first periodic table in 1869. As scientists learned more about the elements, they have revised the table several times. The current version of the table has been in use since the mid-1900s.

Dmitry Mendeleyev was the first of several scientists to contribute to the periodic table.

Molecules: When Atoms Bond

A molecule is the smallest unit of a substance that has all the properties of that substance. For instance, a water molecule is the smallest unit that is still water. It is made up of two hydrogen atoms and one oxygen

A water molecule contains two atoms of hydrogen (H) and one atom of oxygen (O). Here are three ways scientists represent a molecule of water.

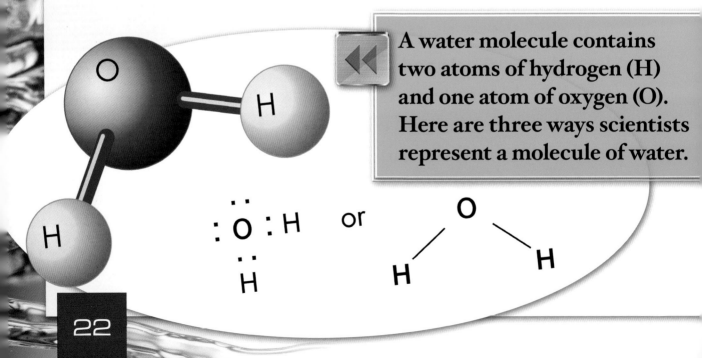

:O:H   or

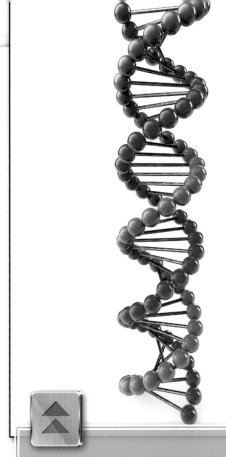

THINK ABOUT IT

Some very complex molecules in living cells are made up of hundreds of thousands of atoms.

atom. But these atoms alone do not have the properties of water.

A strong chemical bond holds the atoms in a molecule together. Bonds form when atoms share electrons. Sometimes electrons are found either alone or in pairs in the outer part of atoms. When two atoms with unpaired electrons approach each other, the unpaired electrons may form a pair. Both atoms then share the pair. This holds the atoms together.

One of the most complex kinds of molecules is DNA, which is part of all living things.

Forces on the Move (or Not)

Physicists study matter and the forces that act on it. In the late 1600s, English physicist Isaac Newton came up with three important laws about matter:

   1. An object at rest will stay at rest unless something moves it. But if an object is moving in a straight line, it will keep moving in the

Physicist Isaac Newton discovered three important laws about motion, or how things move.

Physics is the scientific field that studies matter and the forces that affect it.

same direction at that speed unless another force acts on it.

2. Change of motion is related to the amount of force and takes place in the direction of the straight line in which that force is applied. Kick a soccer ball hard to the left and the ball will go left. Also, a hard kick will move it more quickly than a soft kick.

Which of Newton's laws of motion apply to this picture?

25

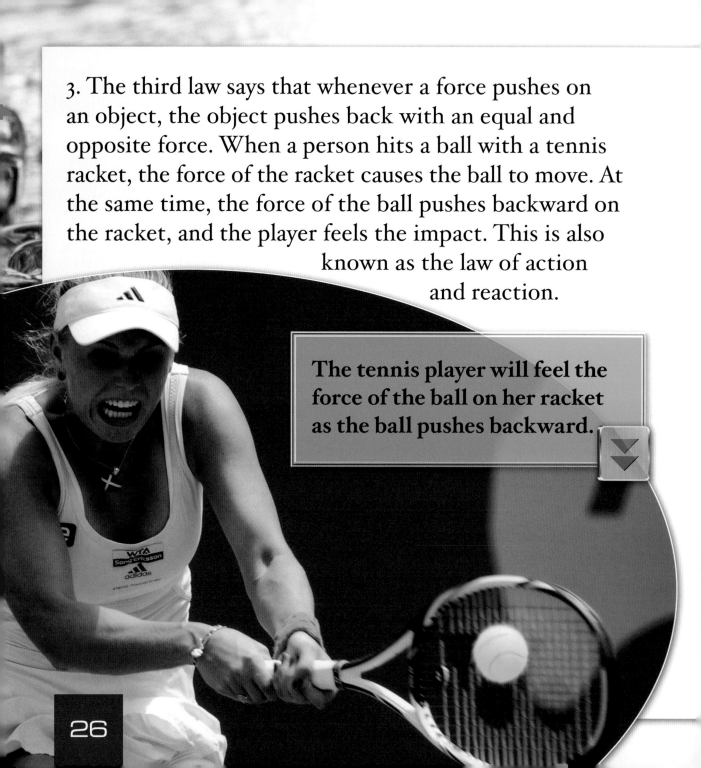

3. The third law says that whenever a force pushes on an object, the object pushes back with an equal and opposite force. When a person hits a ball with a tennis racket, the force of the racket causes the ball to move. At the same time, the force of the ball pushes backward on the racket, and the player feels the impact. This is also known as the law of action and reaction.

The tennis player will feel the force of the ball on her racket as the ball pushes backward.

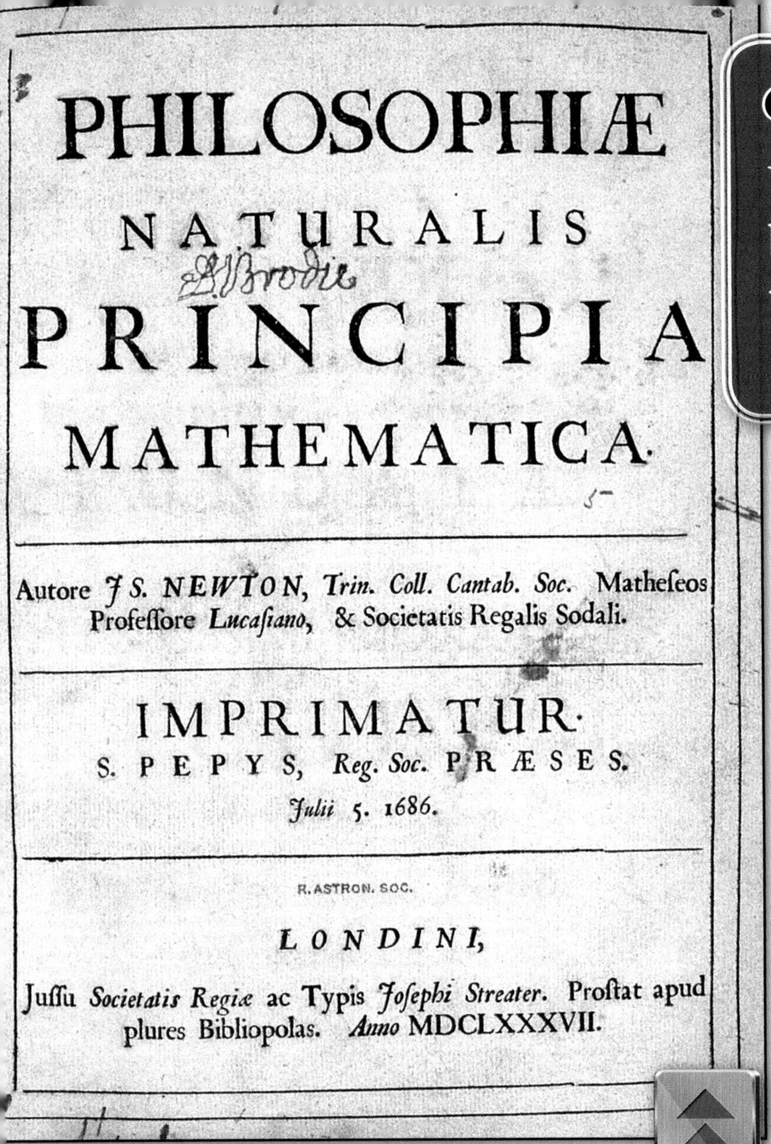

PHILOSOPHIÆ
NATURALIS
ABrodie
PRINCIPIA
MATHEMATICA.

Autore *JS. NEWTON*, *Trin. Coll. Cantab. Soc.* Matheseos
Professore *Lucasiano*, & Societatis Regalis Sodali.

IMPRIMATUR·
S. PEPYS, *Reg. Soc.* PRÆSES.
Julii 5. 1686.

R. ASTRON. SOC.

LONDINI,

Jussu *Societatis Regiæ* ac Typis *Josephi Streater*. Prostat apud
plures Bibliopolas. *Anno* MDCLXXXVII.

Shown here is Newton's classic book explaining his theories about the laws of motion.

COMPARE AND CONTRAST

What is the difference between the first law and the third law of motion?

Today, scientists studying subatomic particles are finding some wild exceptions to these laws, especially for the behavior of matter and light at very small scales. These scientists are called quantum physicists. But for everyday use, Newton's ideas still apply for ordinary objects.

Getting Heavy with Gravity

All objects attract other objects because of a force called gravity. Gravity is a pulling force that works across space. So objects do not have to touch each other for gravity to affect them. For example, the sun pulls on Earth, even though it's millions of miles away.

On Earth, gravity pulls objects toward the center of the planet. This makes objects fall and gives them weight. Weight measures the force of gravity between an object and the surface it stands on. If a person stands on a scale, gravity

Gravity is pulling this drop of liquid toward Earth's center.

THINK ABOUT IT

In a room without air resistance (when air pushes on an object), a feather will fall at the same speed as a brick.

pulls the person against the scale. The scale shows the strength of this force, or the person's weight.

Gravity is what gives weight to objects on Earth. Scales measure the pull of gravity as weight.

GLOSSARY

atomic number The number of protons in the nucleus of a single atom of an element.

atoms The smallest possible units of an element, each of which consist of a nucleus surrounded by orbiting electrons.

bond The force that holds atoms together in a chemical compound.

chemical properties Characteristics of a substance that allow it to change into a different substance.

element A substance that cannot become simpler by any chemical reaction. Elements are the building blocks of all matter.

force A push or a pull acting upon an object.

gas A state of matter that does not have either a set size or a set shape.

gravity A pulling force that works across space.

liquid A state of matter that changes shape according to the container it's in but keeps its volume.

mass A basic property of all physical objects that causes them to have weight.

molecule A chemically bonded group of two or more atoms.

nucleus The center of an atom; the part of an atom made of up of protons and neutrons.

periodic table A system for organizing the chemical elements.

solid A state of matter in which objects hold their shape.

subatomic particles Particles that are smaller than an atom, including protons, neutrons, and electrons.

weight A measurement of the force of gravity acting upon an object.

For More Information

Books

Adams, Tom. *Super Science: Matter Matters!* Somerville, MA: Templar, 2012.

Basher, Simon. *Basher Science: Extreme Physics*. New York, NY: Kingfisher, 2013.

Biskup, Agnieszka, Cynthia Martin, and Barbara Schulz. *The Solid Truth About States of Matter with Max Axiom, Super Scientist*. North Mankato, MN: Capstone, 2009.

Hawkins, Jay. *Push and Pull: The Science of Forces*. New York, NY: Rosen Publishing, 2013.

Hawkins, Jay. *The Science of Matter*. New York, NY: Rosen Publishing, 2013.

Websites

Because of the changing nature of Internet links, Rosen Publishing has developed an online list of websites related to the subject of this book. This site is updated regularly. Please use this link to access the list:

http://www.rosenlinks.com/lfo/matter

INDEX